Searchlight
BOOKS™

Fake News

What Is Propaganda?

Matt Doeden

Lerner Publications ◆ Minneapolis

Lerner Publications Company
An imprint of Lerner Publishing Group, Inc.
241 First Avenue North
Minneapolis, MN 55401 USA

For reading levels and more information, look up this title at www.lernerbooks.com.

Main body text set in Adrianna Regular.
Typeface provided by Chank.

Library of Congress Cataloging-in-Publication Data

Names: Doeden, Matt, author.
Title: What is propaganda? / Matt Doeden.
Description: Minneapolis : Lerner Publications, [2020] | Series: Searchlight books.
    Fake news | Audience: Ages 8–11. | Audience: Grades 4–6. | Includes bibliographical
    references and index.
Identifiers: LCCN 2018057824 (print) | LCCN 2019007428 (ebook) |
    ISBN 9781541556669 (eb pdf) | ISBN 9781541555761 (lib. bdg. :alk. paper) |
    ISBN 9781541574755 (pbk. :alk. paper)
Subjects: LCSH: Propaganda—Juvenile literature. | Fake news—Juvenile literature.
Classification: LCC P301.5.P73 (ebook) | LCC P301.5.P73 D64 2020 (print) |
    DDC 303.3/75--dc23

LC record available at https://lccn.loc.gov/2018057824

Manufactured in the United States of America
1-46031-43354-4/3/2019

Contents

PAGE PLUS Scan QR codes throughout for more content!

Chapter 1

WHAT IS PROPAGANDA?

Since the late 1940s, a Communist government had controlled Poland. In 1989, an opposing party hoped to change that. The party's weapon was propaganda, and it came in the form of a poster.

The Solidarity social movement in Poland brought millions of citizens together in a nonviolent protest against Communism.

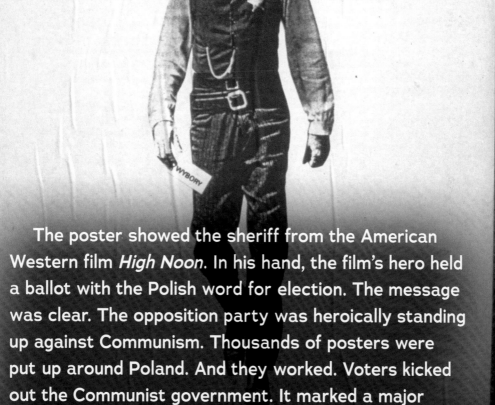

The poster showed the sheriff from the American Western film *High Noon*. In his hand, the film's hero held a ballot with the Polish word for election. The message was clear. The opposition party was heroically standing up against Communism. Thousands of posters were put up around Poland. And they worked. Voters kicked out the Communist government. It marked a major change in Poland—and Eastern Europe. Some called it

Propaganda Basics

Propaganda is information crafted to form or change opinions about a topic. It often appeals to people's emotions. It stirs up feelings, such as patriotism, fear, or anger, to urge people to believe in an idea.

Propaganda is different from news because its creators are not trying to be objective. Propaganda does not present all sides of an argument. Some forms of propaganda are lies. Others present facts in ways that could be misleading or confusing.

This propaganda poster from World War II uses cartoon characters to represent the Germans defeating the British.

However, not all propaganda is untrue. For example, during World War I (1914–1918) and World War II (1939–1945), posters urged Americans to grow victory gardens. The message was that if people grew their own food, more could be sent to the troops overseas.

The information in the posters was true because facts are true by nature. But it was propaganda because it stirred up feelings of patriotism to get people to take action.

Get behind
the Girl he left behind him

Join the land army

During World War I and World War II, Americans were encouraged to grow victory gardens.

Is Propaganda Harmful?

Many people think propaganda is bad, and often it is. During World War II, some propaganda showed Japanese Americans as dangerous and preparing to attack the United States. It was designed to scare other US citizens. It also built support for putting Japanese Americans in camps and preventing them from leaving until after the war ended.

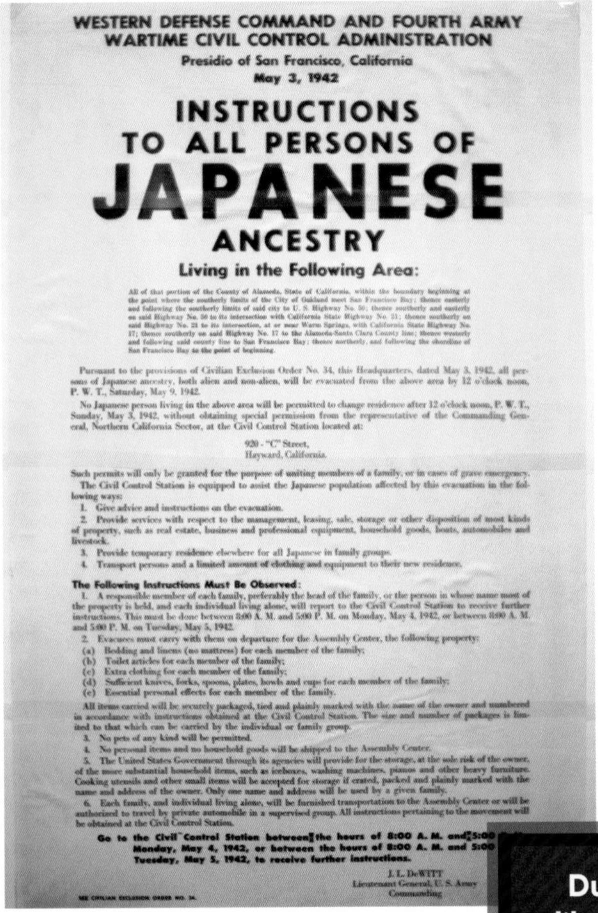

WESTERN DEFENSE COMMAND AND FOURTH ARMY
WARTIME CIVIL CONTROL ADMINISTRATION
Presidio of San Francisco, California
May 3, 1942

INSTRUCTIONS
TO ALL PERSONS OF
JAPANESE
ANCESTRY
Living in the Following Area:

All of that portion of the County of Alameda, State of California, within the boundary beginning at the point where the southerly limits of the City of Oakland meet San Francisco Bay; thence easterly and following the southerly limits of said city to U. S. Highway No. 50; thence southerly and easterly on said Highway No. 50 to its intersection with California State Highway No. 21; thence southerly on said Highway No. 21 to its intersection, at or near Warm Springs, with California State Highway No. 17; thence southerly on said Highway No. 17 to the Alameda-Santa Clara County line; thence westerly and following said county line to San Francisco Bay; thence northerly, and following the shoreline of San Francisco Bay to the point of beginning.

Pursuant to the provisions of Civilian Exclusion Order No. 34, this Headquarters, dated May 3, 1942, all persons of Japanese ancestry, both alien and non-alien, will be evacuated from the above area by 12 o'clock noon, P. W. T., Saturday, May 9, 1942.

No Japanese person living in the above area will be permitted to change residence after 12 o'clock noon, P. W. T., Sunday, May 3, 1942, without obtaining special permission from the representative of the Commanding General, Northern California Sector, at the Civil Control Station located at:

920 - "C" Street,
Hayward, California.

Such permits will only be granted for the purpose of uniting members of a family, or in cases of grave emergency.

The Civil Control Station is equipped to assist the Japanese population affected by this evacuation in the following ways:

1. Give advice and instructions on the evacuation.
2. Provide services with respect to the management, leasing, sale, storage or other disposition of most kinds of property, such as real estate, business and professional equipment, household goods, boats, automobiles and livestock.
3. Provide temporary residence elsewhere for all Japanese in family groups.
4. Transport persons and a limited amount of clothing and equipment to their new residence.

The Following Instructions Must Be Observed:

1. A responsible member of each family, preferably the head of the family, or the person in whose name most of the property is held, and each individual living alone, will report to the Civil Control Station to receive further instructions. This must be done between 8:00 A. M. and 5:00 P. M. on Monday, May 4, 1942, or between 8:00 A. M. and 5:00 P. M. on Tuesday, May 5, 1942.
2. Evacuees must carry with them on departure for the Assembly Center, the following property:
(a) Bedding and linens (no mattress) for each member of the family;
(b) Toilet articles for each member of the family;
(c) Extra clothing for each member of the family;
(d) Sufficient knives, forks, spoons, plates, bowls and cups for each member of the family;
(e) Essential personal effects for each member of the family.

All items carried will be securely packaged, tied and plainly marked with the name of the owner and numbered in accordance with instructions obtained at the Civil Control Station. The size and number of packages is limited to that which can be carried by the individual or family group.

3. No pets of any kind will be permitted.
4. No personal items and no household goods will be shipped to the Assembly Center.
5. The United States Government through its agencies will provide for the storage, at the sole risk of the owner, of the more substantial household items, such as iceboxes, washing machines, pianos and other heavy furniture. Cooking utensils and other small items will be accepted for storage if crated, packed and plainly marked with the name and address of the owner. Only one name and address will be used by a given family.
6. Each family, and individual living alone, will be furnished transportation to the Assembly Center or will be authorized to travel by private automobile in a supervised group. All instructions pertaining to the movement will be obtained at the Civil Control Station.

Go to the Civil Control Station between the hours of 8:00 A. M. and 5:00 Monday, May 4, 1942, or between the hours of 8:00 A. M. and 5:00 Tuesday, May 5, 1942, to receive further instructions.

J. L. DeWITT
Lieutenant General, U. S. Army
Commanding

SEE CIVILIAN EXCLUSION ORDER NO. 34.

During World War II, posters like these instructed Japanese Americans to report to isolated communities called internment camps against their will.

POLITICAL ADS LIKE THE ONE SHOWN HERE
PLAY ON PEOPLE'S FEARS TO GET THEM TO
VOTE FOR AN OPPOSING CANDIDATE.

Other cases are less clear. Political ads use propaganda to affect how people think. Voters may be warned that a candidate doesn't care about children or will let criminals out of jail. These ads may use quotes out of context, or they may provide incomplete data. Their aim is to stir up emotions to affect how people vote.

Real or Fake?

Is this story real or fake? See the Fake News Toolkit on page 29 to help you decide.

Vote Republican and Beat Terrorism

Terrorists want US voters to elect Hillary Clinton. Leaders of the terrorist group ISIS recently supported Clinton in the 2016 presidential election. ISIS leaders even threatened anyone voting for Trump.

Don't let the terrorists win!

Like   Comment   Share

Fake! Social media sites were full of stories like this during the 2016 election. It's made-up. An internet search would reveal that no trustworthy media sources reported it. The story provides no sources and clearly appeals to fear.

Scan the QR code to try another example.

Chapter 2

PROPAGANDA IN HISTORY

The history of propaganda dates back centuries, but it really took off when the printing press was invented in the fifteenth century. Suddenly, propaganda could be produced in large quantities.

After Johannes Gutenberg invented the printing press in the fifteenth century, books and other paper materials could be printed quickly and easily.

Propaganda and War

Nations soon learned the value of propaganda in wartime. During the American Civil War (1861–1865), the Northern (Union) states fought the Southern (Confederate) states. Northern propaganda painted Southerners as cruel slave owners.

THE EAGLE'S NEST.
"THE UNION: IT MUST AND SHALL BE PRESERVED."

This propaganda poster from the Civil War stirs up patriotism for the Union and refers to the Confederate states as traitors.

THE NORTH AND THE SOUTH WERE ENEMIES DURING THE AMERICAN CIVIL WAR, BUT THEY BOTH USED PROPAGANDA TO STIR UP EMOTIONS.

Southern propaganda stirred up feelings of pride for the Confederate army. The North was painted as a threat to the South's way of life.

Propaganda was never more widely used than during World War II. Nazi Germany used everything from film to music to promote its message. German newspapers ran cartoons that presented white Germans as a "master race."

Adolf Hitler believed in a master race of Germans. He described his plans for Germany in his book *Mein Kampf*.

The image of Uncle Sam was used to stir up feelings of patriotism during World War I and World War II.

The United States used the cartoon figure Uncle Sam as a propaganda tool. Dressed in red, white, and blue, Uncle Sam declared, "I Want You!" to convince young men to join the military.

This is your brain,

this is drugs.

this is your brain on drugs.

Partnership For A Drug-Free America   N.Y., NY 10017

Client: Partnership for a Drug-Free America
Job # : 40-235-AD
Size : 7" x 10"
Code : DIPM-2127
Media : TBD

Prepared by keye/donna/pearlstein

Social Propaganda

Propaganda isn't just about war. It plays a role in all areas of culture. For example, in a famous antidrug campaign of the 1980s, a television public service announcement (PSA) showed an egg. "This is your brain," explained the narrator. An image of a frying pan followed with the narrator saying, "This is drugs." Then he cracked the egg into the hot frying pan. As it sizzled, he added, "This is your brain on drugs. Any questions?"

Propaganda comes in many forms, including TV commercials.

Chapter 3

PROPAGANDA AND SOCIAL MEDIA

In this century, the rise of social media websites, such as Facebook and Twitter, allowed people to connect in new ways. Such sites quickly became the preferred type of media for sharing propaganda.

Social media differs from the mainstream media in several ways. Newspapers and network TV stations are expected to present news objectively. They are expected to give the full story, including all sides of an issue.

Unless they are presenting an opinion piece, TV and newspaper reporters state the facts of a story without giving their opinions.

White House: North Korea 'stood us up'

📄 North Korea says it's still willing to meet with Trump

📄 Uncertainty in Asia: Trump's withdrawal leaves region reeling

▶ Heard it first from CNN: Reporter broke news to North Korea

📄 Kim Jong Un's great miscalculation?

TOP NEWS

News agencies try to give only objective information in online stories, whereas social media stories may appeal to emotion.

On social media, many groups present news in ways that support only one way of thinking. For example, a group that opposes immigration may post items that present immigrants as dangerous. A group that supports immigration might show pictures of hungry children needing help. Both posts try to use emotion to affect how readers view a subject.

Fake News

The idea of fake news grew with the rise of social media. A 2017 study showed that 67 percent of American adults get at least some of their news from social media. People often share false news stories without considering whether or not they're actually true. Often, they're not. Some are entirely made-up. Others are misleading.

With so many people reading news stories on social media, it's important to know what is real and what is fake.

In 2017, a video showing two boys in a fight went viral. The post claimed that a teenaged Muslim immigrant was attacking a boy on crutches. Many people shared the video to support the claim that immigrants and Muslims are dangerous. But police later learned that the attacker was neither Muslim nor an immigrant. That didn't stop people from sharing the video, and many who viewed it never knew the real story.

Jayda Fransen of a nationalist group called Britain First tweeted out a series of inaccurate videos casting Muslims in a negative light.

Jayda Fransen
@JaydaBF
Deputy leader of Britain First

London

TWEETS
4

FOLLOWING
16

Tweets

Tweets

Jayda Franser
This is my off
website: brita

During the 2016 presidential election, one-sided stories divided Americans who had strong opinions about the candidates.

Social media propaganda is a powerful tool. In 2016, Russian groups set out to disrupt the US presidential election by flooding social media with propaganda. Strongly biased "news" articles were written to drive Americans apart. This made many people aware of the amount of fake news online. It also caused Facebook and other social media sites to change what they allow to be presented as news content.

Real or Fake?

Is this story real or fake? See the Fake News
Toolkit on page 29 to help you decide.

DAILY NEWS

No. 49,725   THE BEST SELLING NEWSPAPER IN THE WORLD   Today's Edition

National - World - Business - Lifestyle - Travel - Technology - Sport - Weather

Eat Less, Live Longer

Hunger is good for your health. A study published in the journal *Nature Communications* shows that eating less helps mice—and people—live longer. Hunger changes the way cells function. They don't age as quickly, and they last longer. So, if you want to live longer, eat less!

View from the top

Lorem ipsum dolor sit amet, Consectetur adipiscing elit. Vivamus sit amet odio id lorem blandit luctus. Vivamus placerat viverra lorem. Vestibulum consectetur nunc vel sem laoreet dignissim. Cum sociis natoque penatibus et magnis dis parturient montes.

Consectetur adipiscing elit. Vi-

The best way to get something done is to begin

Donec sed turpis ligula. Vestibulum vitae dignissim eros, quis scelerisque lectus. Donec blandit

"Morbi lobortis lacinia, elit in suspendisse egestis, ullamcorper ligula erat,

Economy

Vivamus est elit, tristique id sollicitudin id, mattis et dolor. Morbi lobortis lacinia elit in euismod.

Real! It's true. Reducing calories in a responsible and healthy way does change how your body ages. Studies have shown this in mice, and research shows that it works for people too. How can you tell this story is real? The article gives a source for its information, a scientific journal. That's a good clue that you can trust what you're reading.

Scan the QR code to try another example.

Chapter 4

SPOTTING PROPAGANDA

We live in an information age. From TV to newspapers to the internet, news is everywhere. But not all news is created equally. It is up to each of us to understand what is real and what is not. Everyone should be a skeptic. That doesn't mean we should disbelieve everything. It does mean that we shouldn't accept everything we read, see, or hear as fact.

It can be hard to figure out what is a true story and what is fake news or propaganda. Just remember that not everything you see on the internet is true.

Suppose you see a story on social media about a political candidate. The story tells how the candidate wants to ban the use of plastics in all consumer products. It lists examples of how the laws the candidate supports will take away people's freedom to buy and use all items made of plastic. It may be convincing. It may make you feel surprised or even angry. But is it true?

As we learn more about how plastic bags are bad for the environment, many people feel they should be banned—but most people aren't calling for a ban on all plastic.

WHILE DISCUSSIONS OF BANNING
PLASTIC BAGS ARE FAIRLY COMMON,
DISCUSSIONS OF BANNING PLASTIC
ALTOGETHER ARE NOT.

Ask yourself about the source of the information. Is it from a source you can trust? Does the story include complete information? Are the story's facts backed up by trustworthy sources? Is the writer trying to inform in an unbiased way? If the answer to any of these questions is no, it might be propaganda.

Looking at Bias

We should look for bias in any news we see or read. But we should also be aware of our own personal biases. A variety of media outlets present only the stories that back up opinions we already hold. This can make us less flexible in our thinking. It can cause us to overlook our own biases.

Can you figure out which stories you come across are real and which ones are fake?

You can't avoid propaganda. It's part of our culture. But if we know how to spot it, we can help break the cycle. We can focus on what is real and important and push the fake news aside.

One of these papers is the real *Washington Post*. The other is not. Which one do you think is the phony?

Real or Fake?

Is this story real or fake? See the Fake News Toolkit on page 29 to help you decide.

NEWS | [Search] | **Friday, February 22**

FRONT PAGE | NEWS | SPORTS | VARIETY | LIFESTYLE | COMICS | WANT ADS

EXPOSING GOVERNMENT!

Breaking news! Human beings have never walked on the moon. Documents not yet available to the public prove that the 1969 moon landing was a hoax. It was all staged on a film set. Even one of the astronauts on the mission admitted it. For his protection, his name is being withheld.

Fake! Some people believe this is true. But the story here gives you plenty of reasons to doubt it. The documents aren't available to the public, so they can't be checked. Plus, the astronaut is unnamed, and none of the story's sources can be checked. You can toss this one out as fake news without a second thought.

Scan the QR code to try another example.